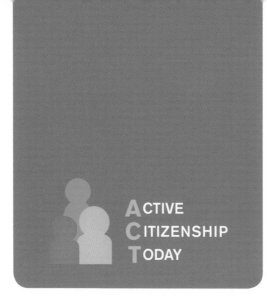

ACTIVE
CITIZENSHIP
TODAY

Challenging Stereotypes and Prejudices

Jeanne Marie Ford

Cavendish Square

New York

Published in 2018 by Cavendish Square Publishing, LLC
243 5th Avenue, Suite 136, New York, NY 10016

Copyright © 2018 by Cavendish Square Publishing, LLC

First Edition

Website: cavendishsq.com

Library of Congress Cataloging-in-Publication Data

Names: Ford, Jeanne Marie.
Title: Challenging stereotypes and prejudices / Jeanne Marie Ford.
Description: New York : Cavendish Square Publishing, 2018. |
Series: Active citizenship today | Includes index.
Identifiers: LCCN ISBN 9781502629166 (pbk.) | ISBN 9781502629180 (library bound) | ISBN 9781502629173 (6 pack) | ISBN 9781502629197 (ebook)
Subjects: LCSH: Stereotypes (Social psychology)--Juvenile literature. | Prejudices--Juvenile literature. | Discrimination--Juvenile literature.
Classification: LCC BF575.P9 F68 2018 | DDC 158.2--dc23

Editorial Director: David McNamara
Editor: Fletcher Doyle
Copy Editor: Nathan Heidelberger
Associate Art Director: Amy Greenan
Designer: Joe Parenteau
Production Coordinator: Karol Szymczuk
Photo Research: J8 Media

Printed in the United States of America

CONTENTS

What Are Stereotypes and Prejudice?

Ruth Bader Ginsburg graduated from Columbia Law School in 1959. She was the top student in her class. However, law firms didn't want to hire her. They didn't want a Jewish woman with a young daughter. She did find work teaching law. Then she had to hide her second

Opposite: Ruth Bader Ginsburg has always challenged stereotypes, including as a justice on the Supreme Court.

Fast Fact!

Nearly 90 percent of LGBTQ students say that they have been bullied at school.

pregnancy. If the college found out, she would lose her job. She had her son during summer vacation. She has fought laws that are unfair to women and minorities. In 1993, she became the second female Supreme Court justice.

Challenging Ideas

Some people believe old ideas about men and women that are not true. They believe that men are smarter than women. They think women are too emotional. They think women do not do stressful work as well.

People like Ruth Bader Ginsburg have worked to prove these ideas wrong. Today, there are more women than men in law school in the United States.

People may be stereotyped based on their religion.
Not everyone in a group acts the same way.

Prejudice and Stereotypes

People are put into groups. They are grouped by
age. Gender, race, and religion also set people

apart. The belief that
all people in a group
act the same is called a
stereotype. Stereotypes
are often wrong. Not
everyone in one age
group is lazy. Not
everyone in another

Every senior citizen
is unique.

Making a Difference

HELEN KELLER

Helen Keller was a one-year-old when she got sick. The illness caused her to lose her sight and hearing. Because she could not hear language, she didn't learn to speak. At the time, people who could not speak were called "dumb." No one realized how much they could understand. Keller eventually learned to read, write, and speak. She attended one of the nation's best colleges. After she graduated, she fought against all **discrimination**. She showed the world how much people with disabilities could accomplish.

Challenging Stereotypes and Prejudices

group is good at music. Women can love sports. Men can enjoy cooking.

Stereotypes describe how we may think about people. **Prejudice** describes how we may feel about them. Prejudice means judging something before we experience it. People tend to favor members of their own groups. This is **favoritism.** It may cause them to look down on members of other groups.

Bias is another kind of favoritism. Parents may be biased in favor of their own children. They think their children are cuter than everyone else's.

Parents usually show a bias for their own kids.

The United States has many laws against discrimination. Title IX is part of a law passed in 1972. It requires equal educational opportunities for men and women. Title IX allowed many more women to play sports and attend college.

Discrimination

Prejudice and bias lead to discrimination. Discrimination means treating people unfairly based on our biases. Not serving an African American family at a restaurant because of their race is discrimination. Not hiring someone based on age or a disability is discrimination. Passing laws that affect people of a single religion is discrimination. Not renting an apartment to a gay couple is discrimination. Bullying is discrimination.

Discrimination can lead to poverty, hatred, violence, and even war.

Old laws in some states discriminated against African Americans. They were forced to sit at the back of the bus. They had to give up their seats to white people.

2

Challenging Prejudice and Stereotypes

Researchers believe stereotypes are not all bad. They help us make quick decisions. Most people know that sharks can be deadly. People who see a shark in the ocean swim to shore quickly. Fear of sharks can keep us safe. However, most sharks don't attack humans. Stereotypes make the world seem simpler than it is.

Opposite: Seeing a shark in the water is scary. Getting to shore quickly is smart. However, most sharks do not prey on humans.

Types of Bias

Bias happens when we think a stereotype is always true. Biases don't always seem bad. Some people believe that all Asian students are smart. This is called a positive bias. A positive bias isn't always true. This can hurt people. A kid who is expected to do well in school may fail. A boss looking for smart workers may hire only Asians. The boss may overlook a smart member of another group.

Often, we do not know about our own biases. We don't form them on purpose. These are called **implicit** stereotypes. Children can form a bias

when they are very young. These implicit stereotypes affect how we act. If a neighbor has an unfriendly cat, you might think all cats are unfriendly. You might miss out on having a great pet someday.

Some cats are friendlier than others.

Students may be punished unfairly because of their race or gender.

We can discriminate against people based on our implicit biases. Students of color get punished

by teachers more often than white students for certain behaviors. Judges give harsher sentences to people who look African.

Implicit biases can affect the way we think about others.

A LOOK AT RACISM

In 1968, all of the third graders in Jane Elliott's class were white. She realized that they didn't understand **racism**. They had never experienced it. She decided to teach them. She told them that the blue-eyed students were smarter than brown-eyed kids. The blue-eyed children sat in the front of the classroom and got extra recess. By the end of the day, the favored group started picking on the others. They did better on their schoolwork. Elliott's students learned that prejudice can grow quickly.

It is important to look at news from many sources.

Understanding Bias

People look for **data** that **confirms** what they believe. They are likely to ignore facts that go against their beliefs.

This can create bias. You can fight this by looking at information from many sources. Keep an open mind. This will help you learn.

Education can help fight bias.

Challenging Your Stereotypes

Who are your three best friends? Are they all the same race as you? Most Americans would answer "yes" to this question. Most of us don't spend much time with people from other groups. This is how we form an implicit bias.

Here are ways to fight your prejudices:

1 Make friends outside of your social group.

2 Work to respect classmates and neighbors who are different from you.

3 Learn about different people's experiences.

4 Try new foods and music and discover other cultures.

5 Examine and resist your own biases.

People can learn to appreciate other cultures by trying new foods.

3

Accepting a Challenge

Many people are afraid to talk about prejudice. They think that talking about differences makes them seem bigger. Pretending prejudice doesn't exist won't make it go away. It usually makes it worse.

Opposite: Making friends from other social groups is interesting.

Acknowledging Prejudice

Discrimination is illegal. However, laws don't always make problems go away. Prejudice is still a problem. Discrimination happens every day. One reason it happens is implicit bias.

Job discrimination harms many people.

Project: Dare to Be Different

Every person is unique. We are kinder to others when we think about their problems. We can't know what it's like to be someone else. We can find out how it feels to be different.

Pick a day to stand out. Wear crazy hair or big glasses or your brother's shirt. How did this small difference change your day? How did people respond? How did that make you feel? How might you change your behavior after this experience?

Taking Action

Try to understand the struggles other people face. Does a new student speak another

Standing out on purpose can help fight bias against those who are different.

language? Imagine trying to learn in a different language. Think about how any bias may affect your actions. Remember, one person can't speak for the whole group.

Good citizenship means including others. It means not calling them names or making fun of them. Being respectful is the first step to reducing discrimination.

Push back against bias even if it is hard to do. Thinking about helping another person will make pushing back easier to do.

Young boys like to play with toy cars. Young girls like to play

Some people think that girls won't like to play with cars.

Toys can help to fight against racial stereotypes.

with dolls. This is a stereotype. It may be true for most children. It won't be true for all of them. Sometimes girls have only dolls to play with. They never get the chance to see if they like cars more.

If you're a boy, would you ever try ballet? If not, why? Would you make fun of a boy who dances?

Stereotypes can change over time.

Boys can be excellent ballet dancers.

You can learn that some are just false. Education and experience help. Keeping an open mind helps. If you want to be treated fairly, then care about treating others fairly.

If you feel you are being discriminated against, say something. If you see someone being treated unfairly, say something. Reach out to responsible adults. Gather support from your community. Gather **allies** from outside it.

Finding support from allies is important.

Challenging Stereotypes and Prejudices

Glossary

allies Friends and people who will support you.

applicant A person trying to get a job or a position.

bias Prejudice in favor of or against a group.

confirm To find facts that prove that something is true.

data Facts and statistics that are gathered.

discrimination Unfair treatment of a group of people who are different.

favoritism The act of favoring one person or group over another.

implicit Something that is hidden so you are not aware of it.

prejudice A judgment about someone that is not based on experience.

racism Prejudice against people because of their race.

stereotype The belief that a whole group tends to behave in a certain way.

Find Out More

Books

Kindersley, Barnabas, and Anabel Kindersley. *Children Just Like Me.* London, UK: DK Children, 2016.

Levy, Debbie. *I Dissent: Ruth Bader Ginsburg Makes Her Mark.* New York: Simon and Schuster Books for Young Readers, 2016.

Tonatiuh, Duncan. *Separate Is Never Equal: Sylvia Mendez and Her Family's Fight for Desegregation.* New York: Abrams Books for Young Readers, 2014.

Websites

Prejudice—Not Giving a "Fair Go"

http://www.cyh.com/HealthTopics/
HealthTopicDetailsKids.aspx?p=
335&id=2348&np=286

This website aims to help kids stay healthy and happy by becoming more aware of prejudice.

Understanding Prejudice

http://www.understandingprejudice.org

This website provides a number of links and self-tests on the subject of prejudice.

Your Cool Facts and Tips on Discrimination and Prejudice

http://eschooltoday.com/discrimination-and-prejudice/discrimination-prejudice-stereotype-for-young-people.html

This site provides information about understanding and dealing with discrimination.

Index

About the Author

Jeanne Marie Ford is an Emmy-winning television scriptwriter. She holds a BA in psychology from Johns Hopkins University and an MFA in writing for children from Vermont College. She has written numerous children's books, and she also teaches college English. She lives in Maryland with her husband and two children.